COLLECTIONS From THE HEART

A Sampling of Cherished Country Quilts & Charming Collectibles

By DEBBIE MUMM

D1371867

Quilting tradition draws on the past to create present-day treasures.
These cherished country quilts, wallhangings, and collectibles are sure to become
family heirlooms treasured by generations to come.

TABLE OF CONTENTS

CREDITS:

Designed by Debbie Mumm
Special thanks to my creative team: Kelly Fisher: Senior Editor
Jodi Gosse, Geri Zimmer & Candy Huddleston: Design Department Assistants
Jackie Saling: Art Studio Assistant ❧ Kathy Grabowski: Office Manager
Mairi Fischer & Nancy Kirkland: Hand Quilters ❧ Barros & Barros: Photography
Marcia Smith Design Associates: Art Direction ❧ © 1997 Debbie Mumm, Inc.

1116 E. Westview Court
Spokane, WA 99218-1384

DEBBIE MUMM®

(509) 466-3572
Fax: (509) 466-6919

www.debbiemumm.com

COLLECTOR'S SAMPLER

Finished Size: 21" x 25"

Our homes are filled with eclectic collections of treasures like the tea cup from Great Aunt Minnie, the vase found in an out-of-the-way antique store, and the kerosene lamp that lit the nights after the ice storm. This nostalgic sampler is fun and easy to make, the perfect way to pay tribute to the collector in us all! Read all instructions before beginning and use ¼" seams throughout.

FABRIC REQUIREMENTS

Blocks - Scraps of assorted fabrics (See Cutting the Strips & Pieces for specific sizes for each block.)

Filler Squares and Triangles
  Coordinated scraps or ⅛ yard pieces

Accent Border - ⅛ yard

Crazy-pieced Border
  Coordinated scraps or ⅛ yard pieces

Crazy-pieced Border Foundation - ⅜ yard

Binding - ⅓ yard

Backing - ¾ yard

Lightweight Batting - 25" x 29" piece

Yo-yos and Appliqué Pieces
  Coordinated scraps or ⅛ yard pieces

Sewable Fusible Web - ¼ yard
  See Quick-Fuse Appliqué on page 40.

Notions - Embroidery floss, 4" doily, beads, assorted ceramic and other buttons

CUTTING THE STRIPS & PIECES

Pre-wash and press fabrics. Using rotary cutter and see-through ruler, cut the following strips and pieces. If indicated, some strips will be cut again into smaller strips or pieces. The approximate width of the fabric is 44". Measurements for all pieces include ¼" seam allowance.

TEA CUP

Fabric A (Cup) One 3½" x 3" piece

Fabric B (Background) One 5½" x 1½" piece
  Two 1½" x 3" pieces
  Two 1½" squares
  Two 1" squares

Fabric C (Saucer) One 5½" x 1" piece

Fabric D (Table) One 5½" x 2½" piece

BUTTON JAR

Fabric A (Jar) One 5½" x 4½" piece

Fabric B (Background) Four 1½" squares
  One 3½" x 1" piece

Fabric C (Lid) One 3½" x 1" piece

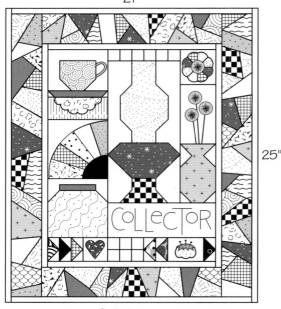

21"

25"

Quilt Layout

LAMP

Fabric A (Shade) One 4½" square
  One 2½" square
  One 2½" x 1½" piece

Fabric B (Background) Four 2½" squares
  Four 2½" x 1½" pieces
  Two 1½" x 4½" pieces
  Ten 1½" squares

Fabric C (Lamp) One 6½" x 3½" piece

Fabric D (Base) One 4½" x 1½" piece
  One 2½" x 1½" piece

VASE

Fabric A (Vase) One 3½" x 4½" piece
  One 3½" x 1½" piece

Fabric B (Background) One 3½" x 5½" piece
  Six 1½" squares

BACKGROUND PIECES

  Fan - One 5½" square
  Heart - One 2½" square
  Dresden Plate - One 3½" square
  Lettering - One 9½" x 3½" piece
  Pincushion - One 3½" x 2½" piece

Filler Squares - Twelve 1½" squares

Filler Triangles
  Fabric A (Triangle) Six 1½" x 2½" pieces
  Fabric B (Background) Twelve 1½" squares

Accent Border - Two 1" x 44" strips, cut into
  Two 1" x 19½" strips and two 1" x 14½" strips

Crazy-pieced Border Foundation
  Three 4" x 44" strips, cut into
      Two 4" x 17" strips and two 4" x 26" strips

Binding - Four 2¾" x 44" strips

MAKING THE BLOCKS

Make one block at a time, referring to diagrams and fabric keys. Refer to Quick Corner Triangle directions on page 39. For each block, corner triangle units are made first and then the block is pieced. Pay close attention that corner triangle units are positioned the same as shown in diagrams. Press seams after each sewing step following direction of arrows in diagrams. It may be helpful to refer to quilt layout on page 2 as you sew. Block details will be added after the quilt top is pieced.

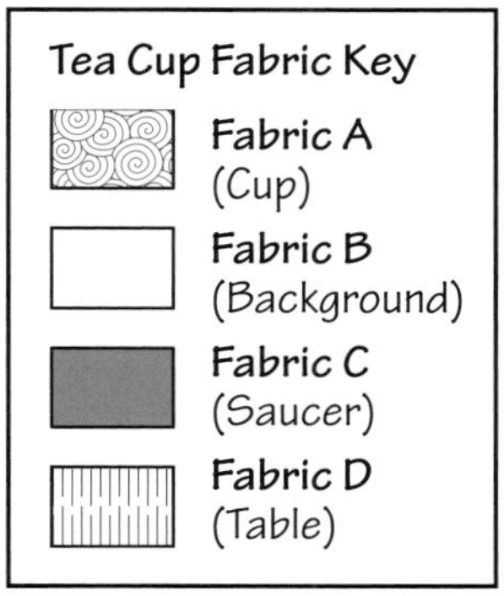

Tea Cup Fabric Key

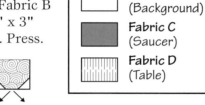

Fabric A	(Cup)
Fabric B	(Background)
Fabric C	(Saucer)
Fabric D	(Table)

TEA CUP

1. Sew two 1½" Fabric B squares to 3½" x 3" Fabric A piece. Press.

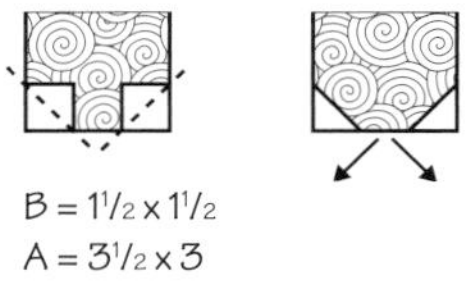

B = 1½ x 1½
A = 3½ x 3

2. Sew two 1" Fabric B squares to 5½" x 1" Fabric C piece. Press.

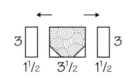

B = 1 x 1
C = 5½ x 1

3. Using ¼" seams, sew corner triangle unit from step 1 between two 1½" x 3" Fabric B pieces. Press.

3   3
1½   3½   1½

4. Sew unit from step 3 between 5½" x 1½" Fabric B piece and corner triangle unit from step 2. Press.

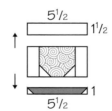

5½   1½
5½   1

5. Center doily on one long edge of 5½" x 2½" Fabric D piece and baste in place. Sew unit from step 4 to Fabric D piece. The doily will be sewn in the seam line. Leaving ¼" seam allowance, trim excess doily from back. Press. Tea cup block will now measure 5½" x 6½".

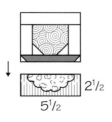

2½
5½

BUTTON JAR

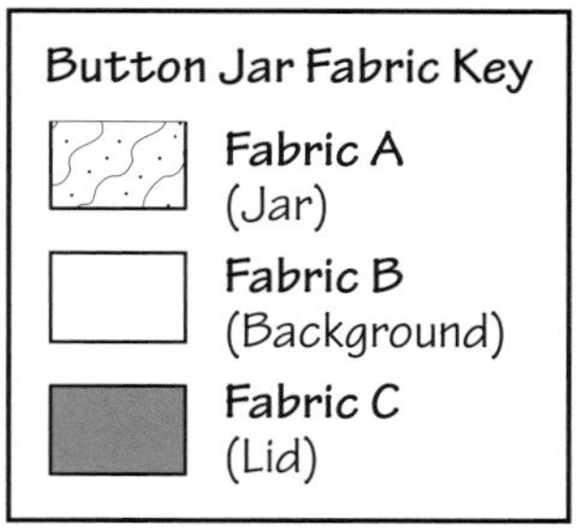

1. Sew two 1½" Fabric B squares to 5½" x 4½" Fabric A piece. Press.

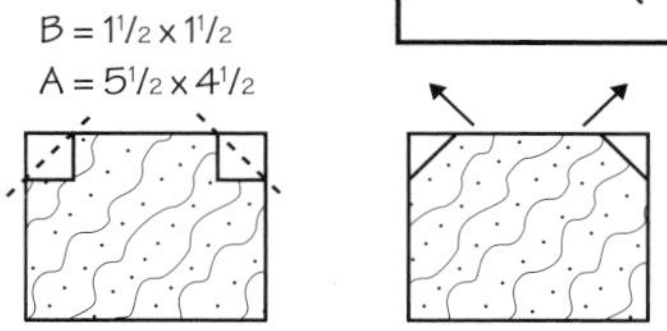

Button Jar Fabric Key

Fabric A	(Jar)
Fabric B	(Background)
Fabric C	(Lid)

B = 1½ x 1½
A = 5½ x 4½

2. Using ¼" seams, sew 3½" x 1" Fabric B piece to 3½" x 1" Fabric C piece. Press.

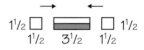

3½   1
3½   1

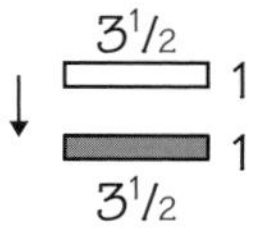

3. Sew unit from step 2 between two 1½" Fabric B squares. Press.

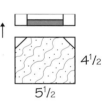

1½   1½
1½   3½   1½

4. Sew unit from step 3 to corner triangle unit from step 1. Press. Button jar block will now measure 5½" square.

4½
5½

FILLER TRIANGLES (SECTION ONE)

1a. Sew three 1½" Fabric B squares to three 1½" x 2½" Fabric A pieces. Press.

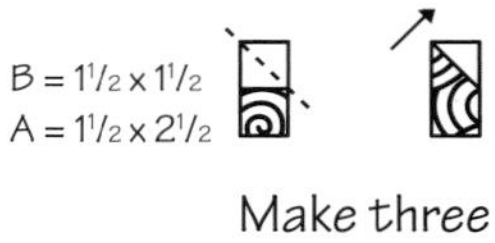

B = 1½ x 1½
A = 1½ x 2½

Make three

1b. Sew three additional 1½" Fabric B squares to units from step 1a. Press.

B = 1½ x 1½
A/B = 1½ x 2½

Make three

2. Using ¼" seams, sew three corner triangle units from step 1b together. Press. Filler triangle unit will now measure 3½" x 2½".

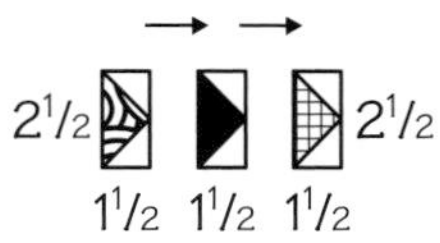

2½   2½
1½   1½   1½

FILLER SQUARES (SECTION TWO)

Using ¼" seams, sew six 1½" filler squares together. Press. Filler square unit will now measure 6½" x 1½".

1½   1½
1½   1½   1½   1½   1½   1½

LAMP

1. Sew four $1^{1}/_{2}$" Fabric B squares to $4^{1}/_{2}$" Fabric A square. Press.

B = $1^{1}/_{2}$ x $1^{1}/_{2}$
A = $4^{1}/_{2}$ x $4^{1}/_{2}$

Lamp Fabric Key

(Shade)	**Fabric A**
(Background)	**Fabric B**
(Lamp)	**Fabric C**
(Base)	**Fabric D**

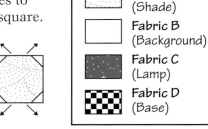

2a. Sew one $1^{1}/_{2}$" Fabric B square and one $2^{1}/_{2}$" Fabric B square to $6^{1}/_{2}$" x $3^{1}/_{2}$" Fabric C piece. Press.

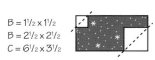

B = $1^{1}/_{2}$ x $1^{1}/_{2}$
B = $2^{1}/_{2}$ x $2^{1}/_{2}$
C = $6^{1}/_{2}$ x $3^{1}/_{2}$

2b. Sew one additional $1^{1}/_{2}$" Fabric B square and one additional $2^{1}/_{2}$" Fabric B square to unit from step 2a. Press.

B = $1^{1}/_{2}$ x $1^{1}/_{2}$
B = $2^{1}/_{2}$ x $2^{1}/_{2}$
B/C = $6^{1}/_{2}$ x $3^{1}/_{2}$

3. Sew two $1^{1}/_{2}$" Fabric B squares to $4^{1}/_{2}$" x $1^{1}/_{2}$" Fabric D piece. Press.

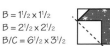

B = $1^{1}/_{2}$ x $1^{1}/_{2}$
D = $4^{1}/_{2}$ x $1^{1}/_{2}$

4. Using $1/4$" seams, sew $2^{1}/_{2}$" Fabric A square between two $2^{1}/_{2}$" Fabric B squares. Press.

$2^{1}/_{2}$ $2^{1}/_{2}$ $2^{1}/_{2}$
$2^{1}/_{2}$ $2^{1}/_{2}$ $2^{1}/_{2}$

5. Sew corner triangle unit from step 1 between two $1^{1}/_{2}$" x $4^{1}/_{2}$" Fabric B pieces. Press.

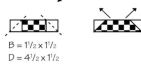

$4^{1}/_{2}$ $4^{1}/_{2}$
$1^{1}/_{2}$ $4^{1}/_{2}$ $1^{1}/_{2}$

6. Sew $2^{1}/_{2}$" x $1^{1}/_{2}$" Fabric A piece between two $2^{1}/_{2}$" x $1^{1}/_{2}$" Fabric B pieces. Press.

$1^{1}/_{2}$ $1^{1}/_{2}$
$2^{1}/_{2}$ $2^{1}/_{2}$ $2^{1}/_{2}$

7. Sew unit from step 5 between unit from step 4 and unit from step 6. Press.

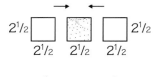

8. Sew $2^{1}/_{2}$" x $1^{1}/_{2}$" Fabric D piece between two $2^{1}/_{2}$" x $1^{1}/_{2}$" Fabric B pieces. Press.

$1^{1}/_{2}$ $1^{1}/_{2}$
$2^{1}/_{2}$ $2^{1}/_{2}$ $2^{1}/_{2}$

9. Sew corner triangle unit from step 3 between two $1^{1}/_{2}$" Fabric B squares. Press.

$1^{1}/_{2}$ $1^{1}/_{2}$
$1^{1}/_{2}$ $4^{1}/_{2}$ $1^{1}/_{2}$

10. Sew unit from step 8 between corner triangle unit from step 2b and unit from step 9. Press.

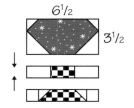

$6^{1}/_{2}$
$3^{1}/_{2}$

11. Sew unit from step 7 to unit from step 10. Press. Lamp block will now measure $6^{1}/_{2}$" x $12^{1}/_{2}$".

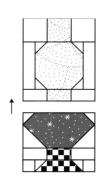

VASE

1. Sew two $1^{1}/_{2}$" Fabric B squares to $3^{1}/_{2}$" x $1^{1}/_{2}$" Fabric A piece. Press.

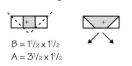

B = $1^{1}/_{2}$ x $1^{1}/_{2}$
A = $3^{1}/_{2}$ x $1^{1}/_{2}$

Vase Fabric Key

(Vase)	**Fabric A**
(Background)	**Fabric B**

2. Sew four $1^{1}/_{2}$" Fabric B squares to $3^{1}/_{2}$" x $4^{1}/_{2}$" Fabric A piece. Press.

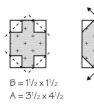

B = $1^{1}/_{2}$ x $1^{1}/_{2}$
A = $3^{1}/_{2}$ x $4^{1}/_{2}$

3. Using $1/4$" seams, sew corner triangle unit from step 1 between $3^{1}/_{2}$" x $5^{1}/_{2}$" Fabric B piece and corner triangle unit from step 2. Press. Vase block will now measure $3^{1}/_{2}$" x $10^{1}/_{2}$".

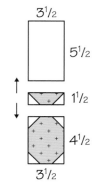

$3^{1}/_{2}$
$5^{1}/_{2}$
$1^{1}/_{2}$
$4^{1}/_{2}$
$3^{1}/_{2}$

FILLER SQUARES & TRIANGLES (SECTION THREE)

1a. Sew three 1½" Fabric B squares to three 1½" x 2½" Fabric A pieces. Press.

B = 1½ x 1½
A = 1½ x 2½

Make three

1b. Sew three additional 1½" Fabric B squares to units from step 1a. Press.

B = 1½ x 1½
A/B = 1½ x 2½

Make three

2. Using ¼" seams, sew two corner triangle units from step 1b together. Press. Remaining corner triangle unit will be used in Putting It All Together, step 7.

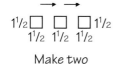

2½ ◣ ◢ 2½
1½ 1½

3. Sew six 1½" filler squares together to make two units with three squares each. Press.

1½ □ □ □ 1½
1½ 1½ 1½

Make two

4. Sew two units from step 3 together. Press.

5. Sew unit from step 4 to unit from step 2. Press. Filler unit will now measure 5½" x 2½".

APPLIQUÉ FAN BLOCK

1. Refer to Quick-Fuse Appliqué directions on page 40. Trace fan from page 7 on sewable fusible web.
2. Quick-fuse fan to 5½" background square, referring to page 7 for placement. With outer edges even, position curved edges of first and last pieces ⅜" from raw edges of background square. Position center last, with straight edges even with raw edges of background square. Outer edges of fan will be sewn into seam.
3. Referring to Embroidery Stitch Guide on page 40, blanket stitch around edges of fan with two strands of embroidery floss.

PUTTING IT ALL TOGETHER

Referring to diagram below, lay out blocks in their proper position. Keep track of layout while sewing blocks together in sections. Use ¼" seams throughout.

1. For Section One, sew fan block between tea cup block and button jar block. Press.
2. Sew filler triangle unit to 2½" heart background square. Press.
3. Sew unit from step 1 to unit from step 2. Press.
4. For Section Two, sew filler square unit to lamp block. Press.
5. Sew 3½" Dresden Plate background square to vase block. Press.
6. Sew unit from step 4 to unit from step 5. Press.
7. For Section Three, sew 3½" x 2½" pincushion background piece between filler unit and remaining 1½" x 2½" corner triangle unit. Press.
8. Sew 9½" x 3½" lettering background piece to unit from step 7. Press.
9. Sew Section Two to Section Three. Press. Sew Section One to Sections Two and Three. Press.
10. Sew 1" x 14½" accent border strips to top and bottom. Press seams toward accent border.
11. Sew 1" x 19½" accent border strips to sides. Press.

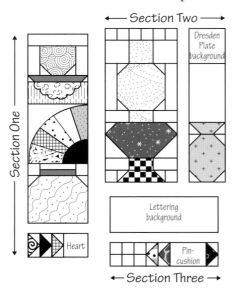

← Section Two →

Dresden Plate background

Section One

Lettering background

Heart

Pin-cushion

← Section Three →

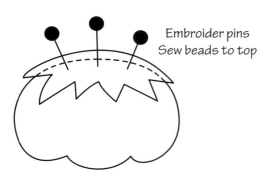

Embroider pins
Sew beads to top

ADDING DETAILS TO THE BLOCKS

Some details are added to blocks before the quilt is quilted. Buttons, yo-yos, and beads will be added after quilting.

1. Refer to Quick-Fuse Appliqué directions on page 40. Trace appliqué designs from pages 5 and 7 on sewable fusible web. Quick-fuse designs to corresponding blocks, referring to color photo on page 20 for placement.

2. Trace lettering and mark other embroidered details, referring to color photo and appliqué designs for placement. Refer to Embroidery Stitch Guide on page 40 to blanket stitch around edges of appliqué designs and to add embroidered details as listed below.
   Blanket stitch - two strands
   Flower stems - three strands, stem stitch
   Lettering - three strands, back stitch
   Pins - two strands, stem stitch

CRAZY-PIECED BORDER

1. Make one crazy-pieced border strip at a time. Position first fabric scrap right side up on top of one 4" x 17" foundation strip. This scrap should be at least as wide as foundation strip.

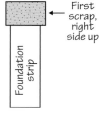

First scrap, right side up

Foundation strip

2. Place second scrap at an angle on top of first scrap, right sides together. Using 1/4" seam, sew along edge of second scrap through all layers.

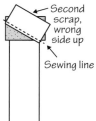

Second scrap, wrong side up

Sewing line

3. Trim first scrap along raw edge of second scrap, being careful not to cut foundation strip.

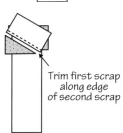

Trim first scrap along edge of second scrap

4. Fold second scrap down and press.

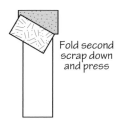

Fold second scrap down and press

5. Continue sewing scraps to foundation until strip is completely covered. To achieve the crazy-pieced look, vary size and placement of each scrap added. Sew scraps to remaining 4" x 17" and two 4" x 26" foundation strips. You will now have four crazy-pieced border strips.

6. Using rotary cutter and ruler, re-cut two shorter strips into two 3" x 15½" strips. Sew to top and bottom of quilt. Press seams toward accent border.

7. Using rotary cutter and ruler, re-cut two remaining strips into two 3" x 24½" strips. Sew to sides and press.

LAYERING THE QUILT

Arrange and baste backing, batting, and top together referring to Layering the Quilt directions on page 39.

FINISHING STITCHES

1. Machine or hand quilt in seam lines of blocks, filler squares and triangles, accent border, and pieces of crazy-pieced border. Outline lettering, stems, and appliqué designs by quilting 1/16" away from edges.

2. Using four 2¾" x 44" binding strips, refer to Binding the Quilt directions on page 39.

3. Refer to Making Yo-yos on page 39. Make three large yo-yos using template on page 7 and sew to flower stems. Make one small yo-yo using template on page 7 and sew to center of Dresden Plate.

4. Sew assorted buttons to jar and border. Sew beads to pins in pincushion.

CERAMIC BUTTON SCOOP...

The charming ceramic buttons featured on this quilt were designed by Debbie Mumm for Mill Hill. Look for these and many other delightful designs in your local quilt shop. If you are unable to find them, see page 40 for ordering information.

#43003	yellow cat
#43014	brown cat
#43021	bonnet
#43024	button heart
#43065	tea cup
#43066	pincushion
#43067	fan

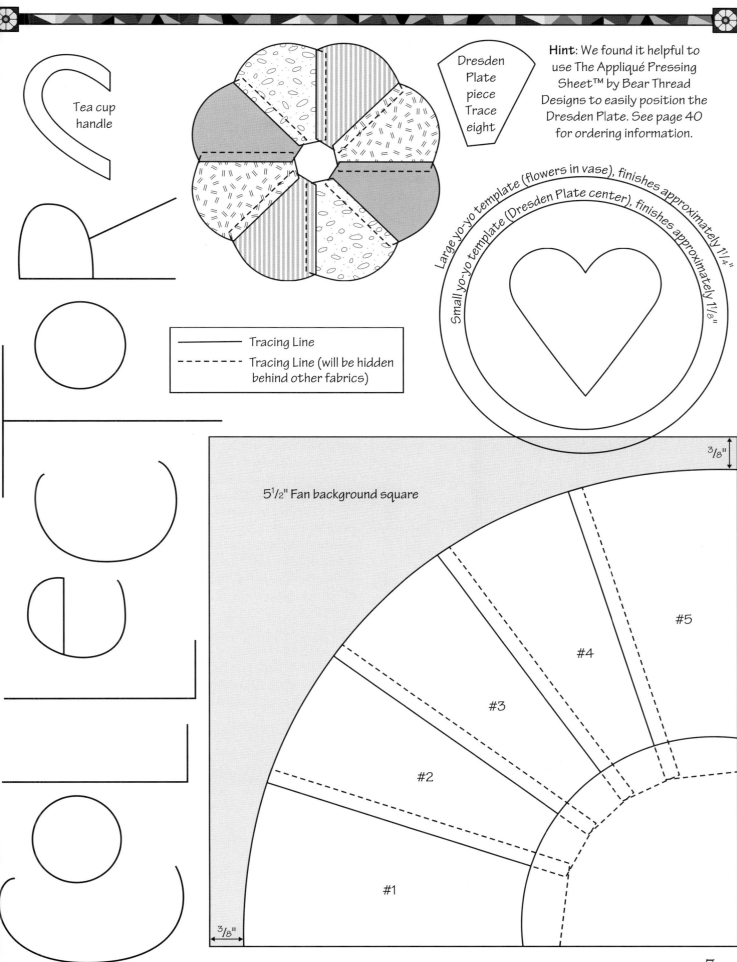

Tea cup handle

Dresden Plate piece Trace eight

Hint: We found it helpful to use The Appliqué Pressing Sheet™ by Bear Thread Designs to easily position the Dresden Plate. See page 40 for ordering information.

——————— Tracing Line

- - - - - - Tracing Line (will be hidden behind other fabrics)

Large yo-yo template (flowers in vase), finishes approximately 1¼"

Small yo-yo template (Dresden Plate center), finishes approximately 1⅛"

³⁄₈"

5½" Fan background square

#5

#4

#3

#2

#1

³⁄₈"

³⁄₈"

GRANDMA'S VASE COLLECTION

Finished Size: 22½" x 19"

Summer visits to Grandma's house meant early morning trips to the garden for flowers to fill her treasured vases and lazy afternoons sipping lemonade while cooling yourself with a hand-held fan. Capture the memories with this quick and easy quilt embellished with doilies, yo-yos, and easy embroidery accents. Read all instructions before beginning and use ¼" seams throughout.

FABRIC REQUIREMENTS

Directional fabrics are not recommended.

Fabric A (Vase) ⅛ yard (or 3½" x 7" piece)
    each of four fabrics
Fabric B (Background) ⅛ yard (or 3½" x 12" piece)
    each of four fabrics
Lattice - ⅛ yard
Accent Border - ⅛ yard
Border - ¼ yard
Corner Squares - ⅛ yard (or 3½" x 16" piece)
Binding - ⅓ yard
Backing - ⅔ yard
Lightweight Batting - 27" x 23" piece
Yo-yos and Appliqué Pieces
    Coordinated scraps or ⅛ yard pieces
Sewable Fusible Web - ⅛ yard
    See Quick-Fuse Appliqué on page 40.
Notions
    Embroidery floss, four 3" doilies (optional)

CUTTING THE STRIPS & PIECES

Read first paragraph of Cutting the Strips & Pieces on page 2.

Fabric A (Vase) One 3½" x 4½" piece
    One 3½" x 1½" piece
    Repeat for each of four fabrics
Fabric B (Background) One 3½" x 5½" piece
    Six 1½" squares
    Repeat for each of four fabrics
Lattice - Three 1" x 44" strips, cut into
    Two 1" x 14" strips
    Two 1" x 11½" strips
    Three 1" x 10½" strips
Accent Border - Two 1" x 44" strips, cut into
    Two 1" x 15" strips and two 1" x 12½" strips
Border - Two 3½" x 44" strips, cut into
    Two 3½" x 16" strips
    Two 3½" x 12½" strips
Corner Squares - Four 3½" squares
Binding - Four 2¾" x 44" strips

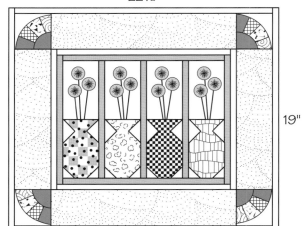

22½"

19"

Quilt Layout

MAKING THE BLOCKS

You will be making four vase blocks, one each of four different fabric combinations. Before you start sewing, coordinate fabrics for all blocks. Keep track of combinations as you sew.

Refer to Quick Corner Triangle directions on page 39. For each block, corner triangle units are made first and then the block is pieced. Use the assembly line method to make enough of the same corner triangle units for all blocks. For each step, position pieces right sides together and line up all sets next to your sewing machine. Stitch first set together and then continue sewing without breaking your thread. Cut threads, trim, and press following direction of arrows in diagrams.

Fabric Key

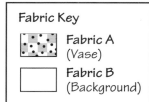

Fabric A (Vase)

Fabric B (Background)

1. Sew two 1½" Fabric B squares to each of four 3½" x 1½" Fabric A pieces (one each of four different fabric combinations). Press.

B = 1½ x 1½
A = 3½ x 1½

2. Sew four 1½" Fabric B squares to each of four 3½" x 4½" Fabric A pieces. Press.

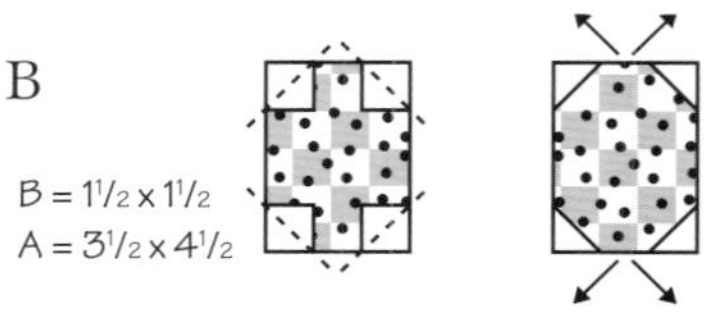

B = 1½ x 1½
A = 3½ x 4½

3. Using ¼" seams, sew four corner triangle units from step 1 between four 3½" x 5½" Fabric B pieces and four corner triangle units from step 2. Press.

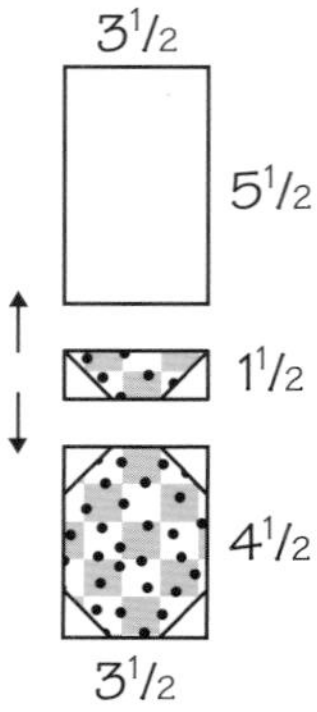

3½

5½

1½

4½

3½

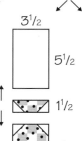

4. Mark three stems on each vase block, referring to color photo on page 22 for placement. Refer to Embroidery Stitch Guide on page 40 to stem stitch stems with three strands of embroidery floss.

LATTICE & ACCENT BORDER

1. Sew 1" x 10½" lattice strips between blocks as shown. Press seams toward lattice. To add optional doilies, center one doily under each vase and baste in place. The doilies will be sewn in the seam line with the bottom lattice.

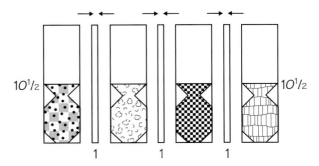

2. Sew 1" x 14" lattice strips to top and bottom. Press. Leaving ¼" seam allowance, trim excess doilies from back.
3. Sew 1" x 11½" lattice strips to sides. Press.
4. Sew 1" x 15" accent border strips to top and bottom. Press seams toward accent border.
5. Sew 1" x 12½" accent border strips to sides. Press.

CORNER SQUARES & BORDER

1. Refer to Quick-Fuse Appliqué directions on page 40. Trace four fans at right on sewable fusible web.
2. Quick-fuse fans to 3½" corner squares. With outer edges even, position curved edges of first and last pieces ⅜" from raw edges of corner squares. Position centers last, with straight edges even with raw edges of corner squares. Outer edges of fan will be sewn into seam.
3. Referring to Embroidery Stitch Guide on page 40, blanket stitch around edges of fans with two strands of embroidery floss.
4. Sew 3½" x 16" border strips to top and bottom. Press seams toward border.
5. Sew 3½" corner squares to each end of two 3½" x 12½" border strips, referring to quilt layout on page 8 for placement of fans. Press seams toward border. Pin and sew borders to sides. Press.

LAYERING THE QUILT

Arrange and baste backing, batting, and top together referring to Layering the Quilt directions on page 39.

FINISHING STITCHES

1. Machine or hand quilt in seam lines of lattice, blocks, and borders. Outline stems and fans by quilting 1/16" away from edges. Quilt a 1½" diagonal grid in border.
2. Using four 2¾" x 44" binding strips, refer to Binding the Quilt directions on page 39.
3. Refer to Making Yo-yos on page 39. Make twelve yo-yos using template below and sew to stems.

Yo-yo template (flowers in vases), finishes approximately 1¼"

JUST FOR FUN
Create a charming patchwork vase from fabric scraps and an old glass vase. Cut scraps into assorted shapes and sizes. Dip in a mixture of equal parts white glue and water. Smooth onto vase forming a crazy patchwork. Let dry thoroughly and spray with acrylic sealer.

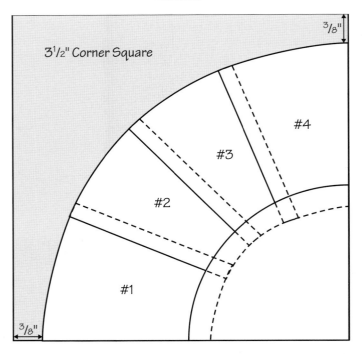

3½" Corner Square

⅜"

⅜"

#1

#2

#3

#4

THE BUTTON COLLECTOR

Finished Size: 18" x 23"

It started with the buttons you found in the drawer of Aunt Estella's sewing cabinet. Then, a neighbor gave you her button box, just because she really wanted you to have it. Soon, you were a button enthusiast, storing buttons in tins and jars. If this sounds familiar, then this fun-to-make quilt is just for you! Read all instructions before beginning and use ¼" seams throughout.

FABRIC REQUIREMENTS

Background Pieces
⅛ to ¼ yard each of eight fabrics
Accent Border - ⅛ yard
Border - ¼ yard
Binding - ¼ yard
Backing - ⅔ yard
Lightweight Batting - 22" x 27" piece
Yo-yos and Appliqué Pieces
Coordinated scraps or ⅛ yard pieces
Sewable Fusible Web - ¼ yard
See Quick-Fuse Appliqué on page 40.
Notions - Embroidery floss, beads, assorted ceramic and other buttons

CUTTING THE STRIPS & PIECES

Read first paragraph of Cutting the Strips & Pieces on page 2.

Background Pieces
Flowers - One 5½" x 3" piece
Lettering - One 2½" x 12" piece
One 2½" x 9" piece
One 2½" x 3" piece
Heart - One 4½" x 3" piece
Pincushion - One 3" x 2½" piece
Cat - One 5½" x 7" piece
Pint Jar - One 5½" square
Quart Jar - One 4½" x 8" piece
Dresden Plate - One 4½" square
Accent Border - Two 1" x 44" strips, cut into
Two 1" x 17½" strips
Two 1" x 11½" strips
Border - Two 3" x 44" strips, cut into
Two 3" x 22½" strips
Two 3" x 12½" strips
Binding - Three 2¾" x 44" strips, cut one into
Two 2¾" x 22" strips

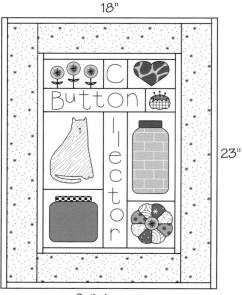

18"

23"

Quilt Layout

BACKGROUND ASSEMBLY

Assemble quilt top before adding appliqué designs. Refer to diagrams for measurements of background pieces. Use ¼" seams and press seams after each sewing step, following direction of arrows in diagrams.

1. Sew 2½" x 3" lettering background between flowers background and heart background. Press.

2. Sew 9" x 2½" lettering background to pincushion background. Press.

3. Sew unit from step 1 to unit from step 2. Press.

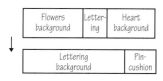

4. Sew cat background to pint jar background. Press.

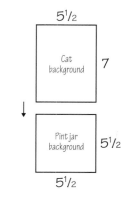

5. Sew quart jar background to Dresden Plate background. Press.

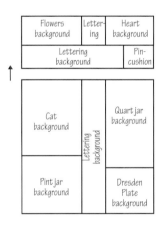

6. Sew 2½" x 12" lettering background between unit from step 4 and unit from step 5. Press.

7. Sew unit from step 3 to unit from step 6. Press.

BORDERS

1. Sew 1" x 11½" accent border strips to top and bottom. Press seams toward accent border.
2. Sew 1" x 17½" accent border strips to sides. Press.
3. Sew 3" x 12½" border strips to top and bottom. Press seams toward border.
4. Sew 3" x 22½" border strips to sides. Press.

APPLIQUÉ & EMBROIDERY

1. Refer to Quick-Fuse Appliqué directions on page 40. Trace appliqué designs from pages 12 and 13 on sewable fusible web. Quick-fuse designs to corresponding background pieces, referring to color photo on page 19 for placement.

2. Trace lettering and mark other embroidered details, referring to color photo and appliqué designs for placement. Refer to Embroidery Stitch Guide on page 40 to blanket stitch around edges of appliqué designs and to add embroidered details as listed below.
   Blanket stitch - two strands
   Flower stems - three strands, stem stitch
   Cat face - three strands, french knots, satin stitch, and stem stitch
   Lettering- three strands, stem stitch
   Pins - two strands, stem stitch

LAYERING THE QUILT

Arrange and baste backing, batting, and top together referring to Layering the Quilt directions on page 39.

FINISHING STITCHES

1. Machine or hand quilt in seam lines around background pieces and borders. Outline lettering, stems, and appliqué designs by quilting ¹⁄₁₆" away from edges. Quilt a 1½" diagonal grid in border, or let your fabric suggest a design.
2. Using two 2¾" x 22" binding strips for top and bottom and two 2¾" x 44" binding strips for sides, refer to Binding the Quilt directions on page 39.
3. Refer to Making Yo-yos on page 39. Make three small yo-yos using template on page 13 and sew to flower stems. Make one large yo-yo using template on page 13 and sew to center of Dresden Plate.
4. Sew assorted buttons to yo-yo flowers, jars, heart, border, above cat, and center of Dresden Plate. Sew beads to flower stems for leaves. Sew beads to pins in pincushion.

CERAMIC BUTTON SCOOP...

The charming ceramic buttons featured on this quilt were designed by Debbie Mumm for Mill Hill. Look for these and many other delightful designs in your local quilt shop. If you are unable to find them, see page 40 for ordering information.

#43033	flying heart
#43036	red circle
#43037	green circle

11

Button It

Tracing Line
Tracing Line (will be hidden behind other fabrics)

Embroider pins
Sew beads to top

12

Dresden
Plate
piece
Trace
eight

Hint: We found it helpful to use The Appliqué Pressing Sheet™ by Bear Thread Designs to easily position the Dresden Plate. See page 40 for ordering information.

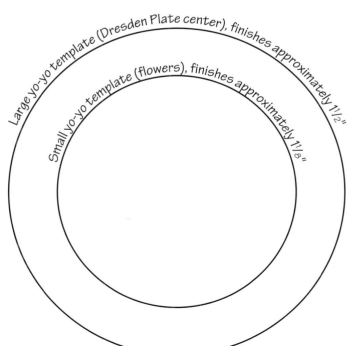

Large yo-yo template (Dresden Plate center), finishes approximately 1½"

Small yo-yo template (flowers), finishes approximately 1⅛"

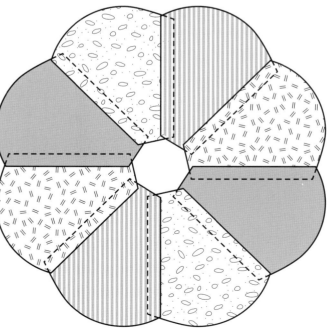

BUTTON...BUTTON...

Finished Size: 20" x $17\frac{1}{2}$"

Gather your favorite buttons. Many are plain, a few are fancy. They all remind us of someone or something special. Spend a relaxing afternoon sorting and sewing them to this easy-to-piece button jar wallhanging. Read all instructions before beginning and use $\frac{1}{4}$" seams throughout. Have fun!

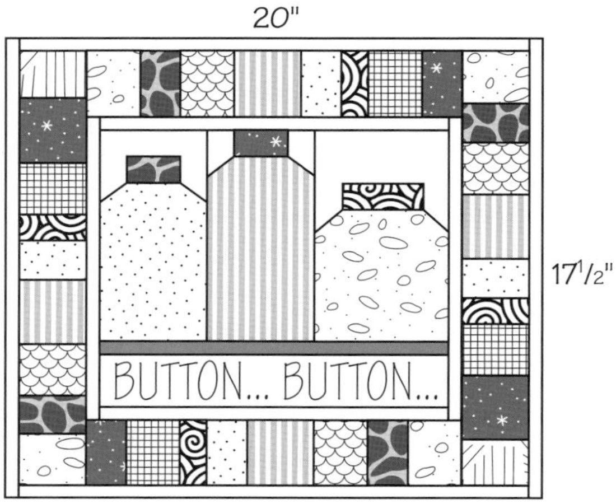
20"
$17\frac{1}{2}$"
BUTTON... BUTTON...

Wallhanging Layout

FABRIC REQUIREMENTS

Fabric A (Jar) $\frac{1}{4}$ yard (or 7" x 9" piece) each of three fabrics
Fabric B (Background) $\frac{1}{8}$ yard (or $2\frac{1}{2}$" x 15" piece) each of three fabrics
Fabric C (Lid) $\frac{1}{8}$ yard (or $1\frac{1}{2}$" x $3\frac{1}{2}$" piece) each of three fabrics
Lettering Background - $\frac{1}{8}$ yard (or $2\frac{1}{2}$" x $13\frac{1}{2}$" strip)
Accent Strip - $\frac{1}{8}$ yard (or 1" x $13\frac{1}{2}$" strip)
Accent Border - $\frac{1}{8}$ yard
Scrap Border - $\frac{1}{8}$ yard (or one strip that measures $1\frac{1}{2}$"–3" wide by 15" long) each of nine fabrics
Binding - $\frac{1}{8}$ yard
Backing - $\frac{5}{8}$ yard
Lightweight Batting - 24" x 22" piece
Notions - Embroidery floss, assorted ceramic and other buttons

CUTTING THE STRIPS & PIECES

Read first paragraph of Cutting the Strips & Pieces on page 2.

Fabric A (Jar) Cut each jar from a different fabric.
- **Left Jar** - One $4\frac{1}{2}$" x $6\frac{1}{2}$" piece
- **Center Jar** - One $4\frac{1}{2}$" x $7\frac{1}{2}$" piece
- **Right Jar** - One $5\frac{1}{2}$" square

Fabric B (Background)
Cut each jar from a different fabric.
- **Left Jar** - Three $1\frac{1}{2}$" x $2\frac{1}{2}$" pieces
  - Two $1\frac{1}{2}$" squares
- **Center Jar** - Four $1\frac{1}{2}$" squares
- **Right Jar** - One $2\frac{1}{2}$" x $3\frac{1}{2}$" piece
  - Two $1\frac{1}{2}$" x $3\frac{1}{2}$" pieces
  - Two $1\frac{1}{2}$" squares

Fabric C (Lid) Cut each jar from a different fabric.
- **Left Jar** - One $2\frac{1}{2}$" x $1\frac{1}{2}$" piece
- **Center Jar** - One $2\frac{1}{2}$" x $1\frac{1}{2}$" piece
- **Right Jar** - One $3\frac{1}{2}$" x $1\frac{1}{2}$" piece

Lettering Background - One $2\frac{1}{2}$" x $13\frac{1}{2}$" strip
Accent Strip - One 1" x $13\frac{1}{2}$" strip
Accent Border - Two 1" x 44" strips, cut into
- Two 1" x $13\frac{1}{2}$" strips
- Two 1" x 12" strips

Scrap Border
- See Scrap Border & Binding directions on page 15.

Binding - Two 1" x 44" strips, cut into
- Two 1" x $19\frac{1}{2}$" strips and two 1" x 18" strips

MAKING THE BLOCKS

Make one block at a time, referring to diagrams and fabric keys. Refer to Quick Corner Triangle directions on page 39. For each block, corner triangle units are made first and then the block is pieced. Pay close attention that corner triangle units are positioned the same as shown in diagrams. Press seams after each sewing step following direction of arrows in diagrams.

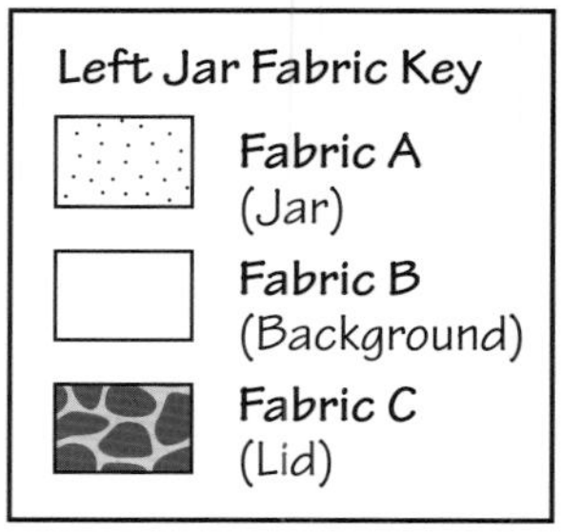
Left Jar Fabric Key
Fabric A
(Jar)
Fabric B
(Background)
Fabric C
(Lid)

LEFT JAR

1. Sew two $1\frac{1}{2}$" Fabric B squares to $4\frac{1}{2}$" x $6\frac{1}{2}$" Fabric A piece. Press.

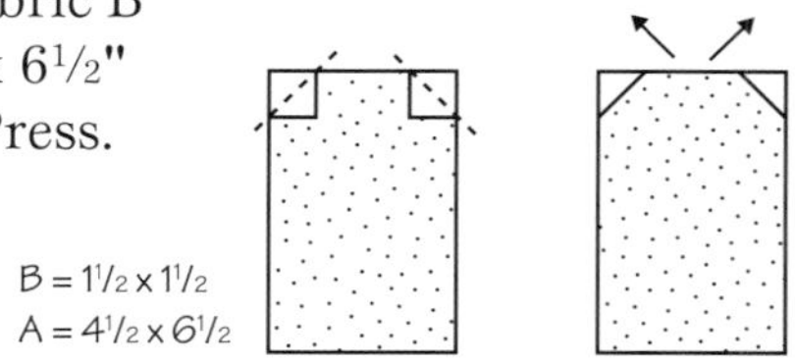
B = $1\frac{1}{2}$ x $1\frac{1}{2}$
A = $4\frac{1}{2}$ x $6\frac{1}{2}$

2. Using $\frac{1}{4}$" seams, sew one $2\frac{1}{2}$" x $1\frac{1}{2}$" Fabric B piece to $2\frac{1}{2}$" x $1\frac{1}{2}$" Fabric C piece. Press.

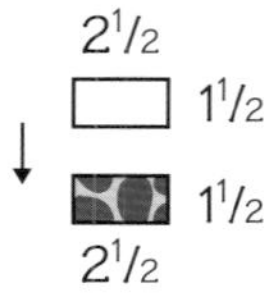
$2\frac{1}{2}$
$1\frac{1}{2}$
$1\frac{1}{2}$
$2\frac{1}{2}$

3. Sew unit from step 2 between two $1\frac{1}{2}$" x $2\frac{1}{2}$" Fabric B pieces. Press.

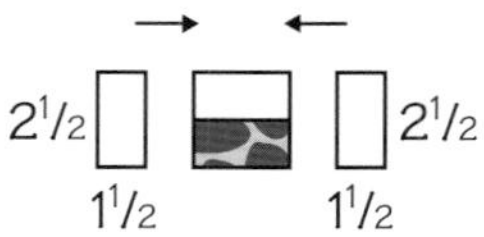
$2\frac{1}{2}$
$1\frac{1}{2}$
$2\frac{1}{2}$
$1\frac{1}{2}$

4. Sew unit from step 3 to corner triangle unit from step 1. Press. Left jar block will now measure 4¹/₂" x 8¹/₂".

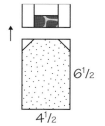

CENTER JAR

1. Sew two 1¹/₂" Fabric B squares to 4¹/₂" x 7¹/₂" Fabric A piece. Press.

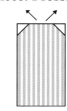

Center Jar Fabric Key	
	Fabric A (Jar)
	Fabric B (Background)
	Fabric C (Lid)

B = 1¹/₂ x 1¹/₂
A = 4¹/₂ x 7¹/₂

2. Using ¹/₄" seams, sew 2¹/₂" x 1¹/₂" Fabric C piece between two 1¹/₂" Fabric B squares. Press.

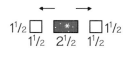
1¹/₂   1¹/₂
1¹/₂ 2¹/₂ 1¹/₂

3. Sew unit from step 2 to corner triangle unit from step 1. Press. Center jar block will now measure 4¹/₂" x 8¹/₂".

7¹/₂

4¹/₂

RIGHT JAR

1. Sew two 1¹/₂" Fabric B squares to 5¹/₂" Fabric A square. Press.

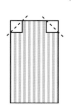 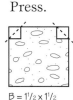

Right Jar Fabric Key	
	Fabric A (Jar)
	Fabric B (Background)
	Fabric C (Lid)

B = 1¹/₂ x 1¹/₂
A = 5¹/₂ x 5¹/₂

2. Using ¹/₄" seams, sew 3¹/₂" x 2¹/₂" Fabric B piece to 3¹/₂" x 1¹/₂" Fabric C piece. Press.

3¹/₂
2¹/₂
1¹/₂
3¹/₂
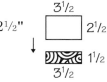

3. Sew unit from step 2 between two 1¹/₂" x 3¹/₂" Fabric B pieces. Press.

3¹/₂   3¹/₂
1¹/₂   1¹/₂
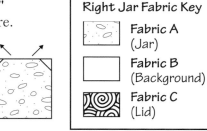

4. Sew unit from step 3 to corner triangle unit from step 1. Press. Right jar block will now measure 5¹/₂" x 8¹/₂".

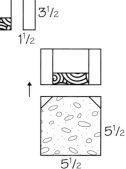
5¹/₂
5¹/₂

ASSEMBLY & LETTERING

1. Sew center jar block between left jar block and right jar block. Press.

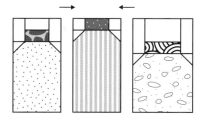

2. Sew 1" x 13¹/₂" accent strip between unit from step 1 and 13¹/₂" x 2¹/₂" lettering background strip. Press.

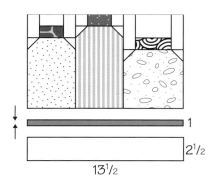
1
2¹/₂
13¹/₂

3. Sew 1" x 13¹/₂" accent border strips to top and bottom. Press seams toward accent border.

4. Sew 1" x 12" accent border strips to sides. Press.

5. Trace lettering from page 16 onto background, referring to color photo on page 19 for placement. Refer to Embroidery Stitch Guide on page 40 to back stitch lettering with three strands of floss.

SCRAP BORDER & BINDING

1. Cut nine 15" strips (one each of nine different fabrics) that vary in width from 1¹/₂"–3". Sew together to make a 17" x 15" strip set. Change sewing direction with each strip sewn and press seams in one direction. Using rotary cutter and ruler, cut four 3" x 17" scrap border strips from this strip set.

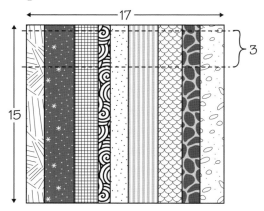
17
15
3

2. Pin and sew scrap border strips to top and bottom. Trim excess length of scrap border strips. Press seams toward accent border.

3. Pin and sew scrap border strips to sides. Press.

15

4. Sew 1" x 19½" binding strips to top and bottom. Press seams toward binding.
5. Sew 1" x 18" binding strips to sides. Press.

LAYERING & FINISHING

1. Position top and backing right sides together. Lay both pieces on top of batting and pin all three layers together. Using ¼" seam, sew around edges leaving an opening for turning. Trim backing and batting to same size as top. Trim corners, turn right side out, hand stitch opening closed, and press.
2. Machine or hand quilt in seam lines around jars, lids, lettering background, accent border, and pieces of scrap border. Outline lettering by quilting ¹⁄₁₆" away from letters.
3. Sew assorted buttons to jars and border.

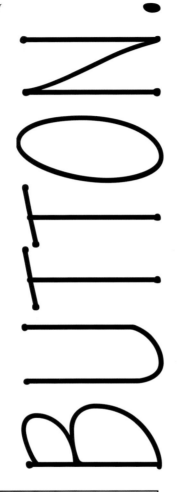

CERAMIC BUTTON SCOOP...

The charming ceramic buttons featured on this wallhanging were designed by Debbie Mumm for Mill Hill. Look for these and many other delightful designs in your local quilt shop. If you are unable to find them, see page 40 for ordering information.

#43002	brown bear
#43003	yellow cat
#43005	sunflower
#43021	bonnet
#43024	button heart
#43032	yellow birdhouse
#43033	flying heart
#43035	gold house

BUTTONS & BOWS WALL QUILT

Finished Size: 26" square

Life is a patchwork of pleasant memories sewn together with love, the old combined with the new. This easy-to-make wall quilt features time-honored blocks combined with today's easy construction techniques. Buttons placed randomly throughout the border add a delightful finishing touch. Read all instructions before beginning and use ¼" seams throughout.

FABRIC REQUIREMENTS

BOW TIE BLOCKS

Fabric A (Bow Tie) ⅛ yard (or 2¾" x 10" piece) each of five fabrics
Fabric B (Background) ⅛ yard (or 2¾" x 7" piece) each of five fabrics
Fabric C (Triangles) ⅛ yard (or 3⅞" x 9" piece) each of five fabrics

CHURN DASH BLOCKS

Fabric D (Triangles) ⅛ yard (or 2½" x 12" piece) each of four fabrics
Fabric E (Background) ⅛ yard each of four fabrics
Fabric F (Rectangles) ⅛ yard (or 1½" x 12" piece) each of four fabrics

Lattice - ⅙ yard
Border - ¼ yard
Patchwork Border - ⅛ yard (or 1½" x 18" strip) each of twelve fabrics
Binding - ⅓ yard
Backing - ⅞ yard
Lightweight Batting - 30" square
Notions - Assorted buttons

CUTTING THE STRIPS & PIECES

Read first paragraph of Cutting the Strips & Pieces on page 2.

BOW TIE BLOCKS

Fabric A (Bow Tie) Two 2¾" squares
Two 1½" squares
Repeat for each of five fabrics
Fabric B (Background)
Two 2¾" squares each of five fabrics
Fabric C (Triangles)
Two 3⅞" squares each of five fabrics

CHURN DASH BLOCKS

Fabric D (Triangles)
Four 2½" squares each of four fabrics

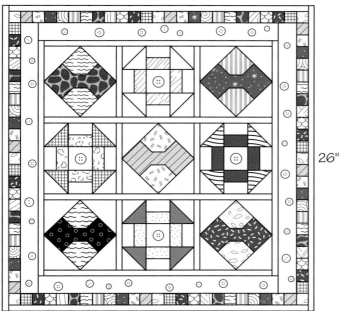

26"

26"

Wall Quilt Layout

Fabric E (Background) Five 2½" squares
Four 2½" x 1½" pieces
Repeat for each of four fabrics
Fabric F (Rectangles)
Four 2½" x 1½" pieces each of four fabrics
Lattice - Five 1" x 44" strips, cut into
Two 1" x 20½" strips
Four 1" x 19½" strips
Six 1" x 6½" strips
Border - Two 2" x 23½" strips
Two 2" x 20½" strips
Patchwork Border
One 1½" x 18" strip each of twelve fabrics
Binding - Four 2¾" x 44" strips

MAKING THE BLOCKS

You will be making five Bow Tie blocks and four
Churn Dash blocks. Each block uses a different
fabric combination. Before you start sewing,
coordinate fabrics for all blocks. Keep track of
combinations as you sew.

Refer to Quick Corner Triangle directions on
page 39. For each block, corner triangle units are
made first and then the block is pieced. Use the
assembly line method to make enough of the same
corner triangle units for all blocks. For each step,
position pieces right sides together and line up all
sets next to your sewing machine. Stitch first set
together and then continue sewing without
breaking your thread. Cut threads, trim, and press
following direction of arrows in diagrams.

BOW TIE BLOCKS

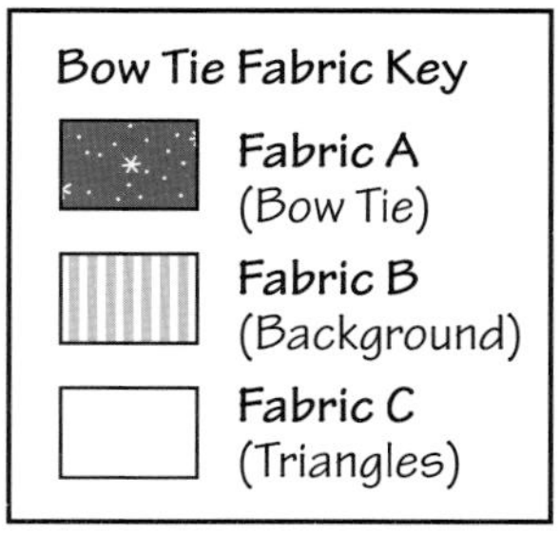

1. Sew ten 1½" Fabric A
squares to ten 2¾"
Fabric B squares (two
each of five different
fabric combinations).
Press.

A = 1½" x 1½"
B = 2¾" x 2¾"

Bow Tie Fabric Key

▨	**Fabric A** (Bow Tie)
▥	**Fabric B** (Background)
☐	**Fabric C** (Triangles)

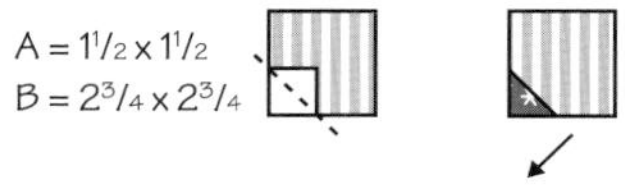

2. Using ¼" seams, sew ten
2¾" Fabric A squares to
ten corner triangle units
from step 1. Press.

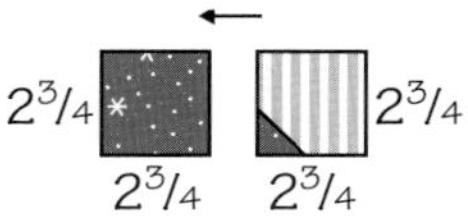

2¾ 2¾
2¾ 2¾

3. Sew ten units from step 2
together in pairs. Press. Using
rotary cutter and ruler,
**trim blocks to measure
4¾" square**.

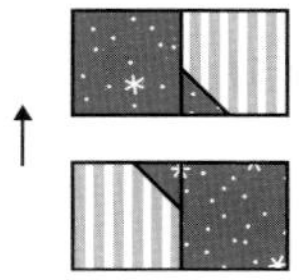

4. Cut ten 3⅞" Fabric C
squares in half
diagonally to make
twenty triangles. Sew five
units from step 3 between
ten Fabric C triangles. Press.

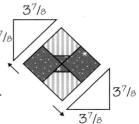

3⅞
3⅞
3⅞
3⅞

5. Sew five units from step 4
between ten remaining
Fabric C triangles. Press.
Bow Tie blocks will now
measure 6½" square.

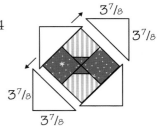

3⅞
3⅞
3⅞
3⅞

CHURN DASH BLOCKS

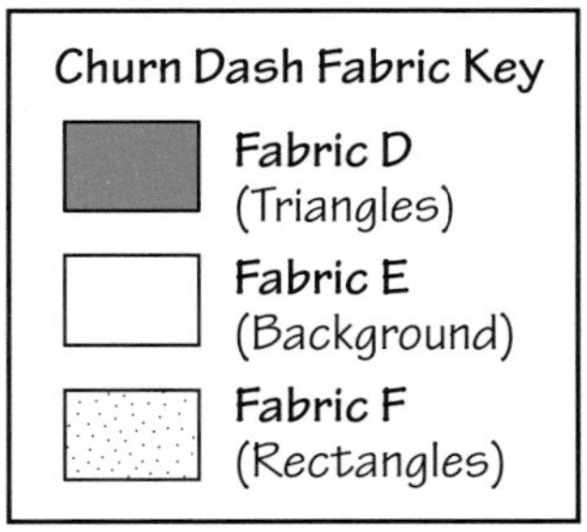

1. Sew sixteen 2½"
Fabric D squares to
sixteen 2½" Fabric E
squares (four each of
four different fabric
combinations). Press.

D = 2½" x 2½"
E = 2½" x 2½"

Churn Dash Fabric Key

▦	**Fabric D** (Triangles)
☐	**Fabric E** (Background)
▨	**Fabric F** (Rectangles)

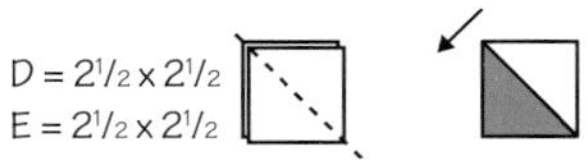

2. Using ¼" seams, sew sixteen
2½" x 1½" Fabric E pieces to
sixteen 2½" x 1½" Fabric F pieces.
Press.

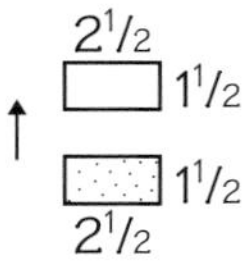

2½
1½
1½
2½

3. Sew eight units from step 2 between sixteen corner triangle units from step 1. Press.

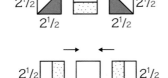

4. Sew four 2¹/₂" Fabric E squares between eight remaining units from step 2. Press.

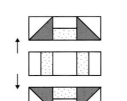

5. Sew four units from step 4 between eight units from step 3. Press. Churn Dash blocks will now measure 6¹/₂" square.

LATTICE

1. Referring to quilt layout on page 17, lay out blocks in a pleasing arrangement. Keep track of your layout while sewing on lattice.
2. For Rows One and Three, sew 1" x 6¹/₂" lattice strips between blocks as shown. Press seams toward lattice. For Row Two, sew lattice strips between blocks as shown. Press.

Rows One and Three

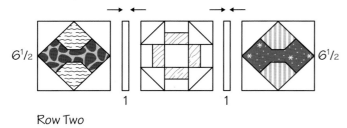

Row Two

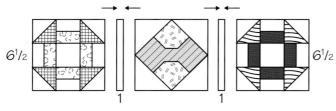

3. Sew 1" x 19¹/₂" lattice strips to bottom of each row and to top of top row. Join rows and press.
4. Sew 1" x 20¹/₂" lattice strips to sides. Press.

BORDERS

1. Sew 2" x 20¹/₂" border strips to top and bottom. Press seams toward border.
2. Sew 2" x 23¹/₂" border strips to sides. Press.

3. Arrange twelve 1¹/₂" x 18" patchwork border strips in a pleasing order. Sew together to make a 12¹/₂" x 18" strip set. Change sewing direction with each strip sewn and press seams in one direction as you go. Cut this strip set in half, approximately 9" each.

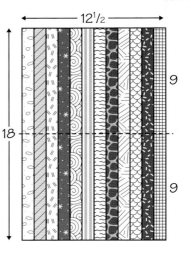

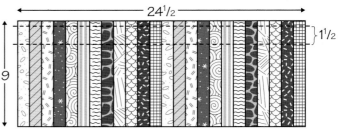

4. Re-sew halves together to make a 24¹/₂" x 9" strip set. Using rotary cutter and ruler, cut four 1¹/₂" x 24¹/₂" strips from this strip set. For top and bottom borders, use seam ripper to remove one square from each of two strips to make two strips with twenty-three squares each. Excess squares will be used in step 5. Compare strips to top and bottom of quilt. You might need to take in or let out a few seams (¹/₁₆" or less) to make them fit. Pin and sew patchwork border strips to top and bottom. Press seams toward border.
5. For side borders, sew one square from step 4 to each remaining patchwork border strip to make two strips with twenty-five squares each. Fit, pin, and sew patchwork border strips to sides. Press.

LAYERING THE QUILT

Arrange and baste backing, batting, and top together referring to Layering the Quilt directions on page 39.

FINISHING STITCHES

1. Machine or hand quilt in seam lines of blocks, lattice, and pieces of patchwork border.
2. Using four 2³/₄" x 44" binding strips, refer to Binding the Quilt directions on page 39.
3. Sew assorted buttons to blocks and border.

The Button
Collector, *p.10*
Small Stuffed Hearts, *p.37*
Button Jar Lamp, *p.36*
Mini Quilt Collection,
p.30

Button...
Button...,
p.14

Collector's Cardigan, *p.33*
Mini Quilt Collection, *p.30*
▶

Crazy-pieced Pillow *p.38*

Collector's Sampler, *p.2*
Pillows At Heart, *p.37*
Small Stuffed Hearts, *p.37*

Grandma's Vase
Collection, *p.8*
Small Stuffed Hearts, *p.37*
Collector Boxes, *p.35*
Mini Quilt Collection,
p.30

▶

Mini Quilt
Collection, *p.30*
Timeless Traditions
Wall Quilt, *p.28*
Sewing Is My Cup
Of Tea, *p.36*

BETSY'S BOW TIE DOLL QUILT

Finished Size: 21" x 25"

Gather a variety of fabrics in hues of red, green, blue, and gold to create a quilt worthy of a child's tender love for her favorite doll. This darling doll quilt combines quick rotary cutting with easy piecing techniques. Read all instructions before beginning and use ¼" seams throughout.

21"

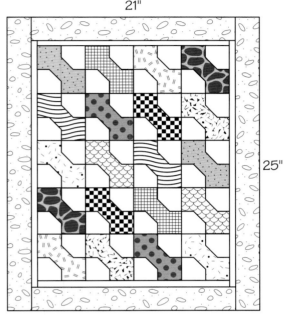

25"

Doll Quilt Layout

FABRIC REQUIREMENTS

Fabric A (Bow Tie) - ⅛ yard each of ten fabrics
Fabric B (Background) - ⅛ yard each of ten fabrics
Accent Border - ⅛ yard
Border - ¼ yard
Backing - ¾ yard
Lightweight Batting - 25" x 29" piece

CUTTING THE STRIPS & PIECES

Read first paragraph of Cutting the Strips & Pieces on page 2.

Fabric A (Bow Tie) Four 2½" squares
    Four 1½" squares
    Repeat for each of ten fabrics
Fabric B (Background)
    Four 2½" squares each of ten fabrics
Accent Border - Two 1" x 44" strips, cut into
    Two 1" x 21½" strips
    Two 1" x 16½" strips
Border - Three 2½" x 44" strips, cut into
    Two 2½" x 25½" strips
    Two 2½" x 17½" strips

MAKING THE BLOCKS

You will be making twenty Bow Tie blocks, two each of ten fabric combinations. Before you start sewing, coordinate fabrics for all combinations. Keep track of combinations as you sew.

Refer to Quick Corner Triangle directions on page 39. For each block, corner triangle units are made first and then the block is pieced. Use the assembly line method to make enough of the same corner triangle units for all blocks. For each step, position pieces right sides together and line up all sets next to your sewing machine. Stitch first set together and then continue sewing without breaking your thread. Cut threads, trim, and press following direction of arrows in diagrams.

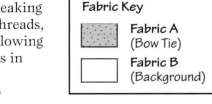

Fabric Key
Fabric A (Bow Tie)
Fabric B (Background)

1. Sew forty 1½" Fabric A squares to forty 2½" Fabric B squares (four each of ten different fabric combinations). Press.

    A = 1½ x 1½
    B = 2½ x 2½

2. Using ¼" seams, sew forty 2½" Fabric A squares to forty corner triangle units from step 1. Press.

    2½ 2½
    2½ 2½

3. Sew forty units from step 2 together in pairs. Press. Bow Tie blocks will now measure 4½" square.

ASSEMBLY

1. Arrange blocks in a pleasing order of five rows with four blocks each. Sew blocks together in rows. Press seams in rows one, three, and five in one direction. Press seams in rows two and four in opposite direction.

2. Sew rows together and press.
3. Sew 1" x 16½" accent border strips to top and bottom. Press seams toward accent border.
4. Sew 1" x 21½" accent border strips to sides. Press.
5. Sew 2½" x 17½" border strips to top and bottom. Press seams toward border.
6. Sew 2½" x 25½" border strips to sides. Press.

LAYERING & FINISHING

1. Position top and 4½" backing square right sides together. Lay both pieces on top of flannel or batting, and pin all three layers together. Using ¼" seam allowance, sew around edges, leaving an opening for turning. Trim corners, turn right side out, hand stitch opening closed, and press.

2. Machine or hand quilt in seam line of border and corner squares. Finish mini quilts as specified below.

DRESDEN PLATE

Refer to Making Yo-yos on page 39 to make one small yo-yo using template below. Sew yo-yo and button to center of Dresden Plate.

HEART

Sew button to center of heart.

BOW TIE

Quilt in seam lines of Bow Tie. Sew button to center of each background square or to center of Bow Tie.

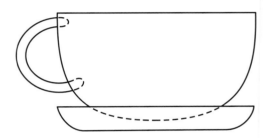

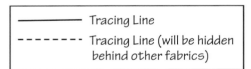

	Tracing Line
- - - - - - -	Tracing Line (will be hidden behind other fabrics)

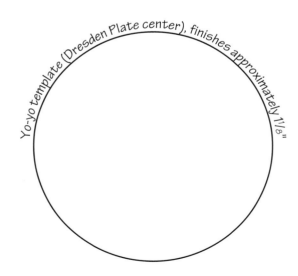

Yo-yo template (Dresden Plate center), finishes approximately 1⅛"

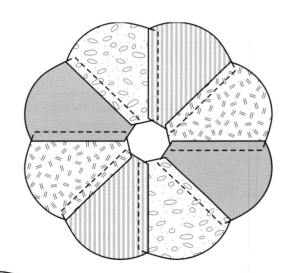

Dresden Plate piece Trace eight

Hint: We found it helpful to use The Appliqué Pressing Sheet™ by Bear Thread Designs to easily position the Dresden Plate. See page 40 for ordering information.

COLLECTOR'S CARDIGAN

Here is our recipe for a charming collector's cardigan. Take one soft and snugly sweatshirt and add your favorite things; quilt blocks, buttons, yo-yos, and charms. Assemble with love and wear with pride!

FABRIC REQUIREMENTS

Center Front Binding - ¼ yard
Bottom Band - ⅝ yard
Pocket Lattice and Lining - ¼ yard
Pocket Corner Squares
     ⅛ yard (or 1" x 14" strip)
Blocks - Scraps of assorted fabrics
Yo-yos and Appliqué Pieces
     Coordinated scraps or ⅛ yard pieces
Sewable Fusible Web - ¼ yard
     See Quick-Fuse Appliqué on page 40.
Pre-washed sweatshirt
Notions - Embroidery floss, #5 perle cotton, ceramic and other assorted buttons, charms, small doily

CUTTING THE STRIPS & PIECES

Read first paragraph of Cutting the Strips & Pieces on page 2.

Center Front Binding - Two 3" x 44" strips
Bottom Band - Two 9" x 30" strips
Pocket Lining and Lattice
     One 8" square (Lining)
     Twelve 1 x 3½" strips (Lattice)
Pocket Corner Squares - Nine 1" squares

MAKING THE CARDIGAN

1. Cut ribbing off bottom of sweatshirt. Find and mark center front of sweatshirt. Cut open on marked center front.
2. Sew two 9" x 30" bottom band strips together to make one 9" x 59½" strip. Fold and press strip in half lengthwise with wrong sides together.
3. Match seam of bottom band to center back of sweatshirt. With raw edges even, pin bottom band to right side of sweatshirt. The ends of the bottom band will extend past the center front of the sweatshirt. Sew through all layers, ¼" from raw edges. Press bottom band away from sweatshirt. Trim excess length of bottom band even with edges of center front.

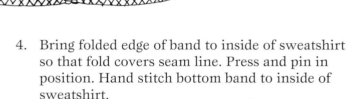

4. Bring folded edge of band to inside of sweatshirt so that fold covers seam line. Press and pin in position. Hand stitch bottom band to inside of sweatshirt.
5. Measure length of center front of sweatshirt, including bottom band. Cut 3" front binding strips to the length of center front plus 1". Fold and press binding strips in half lengthwise with wrong sides together. Using ½" seams and being careful not to stretch sweatshirt, pin and sew binding strips to right side of sweatshirt. Binding strips will extend ½" beyond top and bottom of sweatshirt.
6. Press binding away from sweatshirt. Fold raw edges of binding strips over top and bottom of sweatshirt. Bring folded edge of binding to inside of sweatshirt so that fold covers seam line. Hand stitch binding to inside of sweatshirt.

PATCHWORK BLOCKS

1. Choose three blocks from the Mini Quilt Collection. Refer to Cutting the Strips & Pieces, Making the Center Blocks, and Adding the Border on pages 30 and 31 to make three patchwork blocks without flannel or batting.
2. Referring to Embroidery Stitch Guide on page 40, blanket stitch around edges of Dresden Plate, tea cup, or heart.
3. Omitting flannel or batting, refer to Layering & Finishing on page 32 to back the patchwork blocks and to add finishing details.

MAKING THE POCKET

1. Choose four blocks from the Mini Quilt Collection. Refer to Cutting the Strips & Pieces and Making the Center Blocks to make four blocks without borders, corner squares, flannel, or backing.

2. Referring to Embroidery Stitch Guide on page 40, blanket stitch around edges of Dresden Plate, tea cup, or heart.

3. Lay out your blocks in a pleasing arrangement. Using ¼" seams, sew six 1 x 3½" lattice strips and four 3½" blocks together as shown to make two rows. Press.

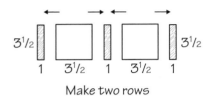

Make two rows

4. Sew six 1 x 3½" lattice strips and nine 1" corner squares together as shown to make three lattice strips. Press.

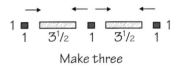

Make three

5. Sew lattice strips to bottom of both rows from step 3 and to top of top row. Press. Join rows and press.

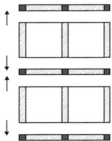

6. Position pocket and lining right sides together. Sew around edges, leaving an opening for turning. Trim corners, turn right side out, hand stitch opening closed, and press.

7. Referring to Layering & Finishing on page 32, add yo-yos and buttons to blocks as desired.

DECORATING THE CARDIGAN

1. Referring to color photo on page 20, position and pin pocket on right front and patchwork blocks on left front. Hand stitch in place.

2. Refer to Making Yo-yos on page 39 to make ten yo-yos using template below.

3. Position and sew buttons to neck of cardigan. Scatter yo-yos, buttons, and charms on front of cardigan. Sew in place.

4. Use #5 perle cotton to sew large running stitch down front and around cuffs, patchwork blocks, pocket, neck, and bottom.

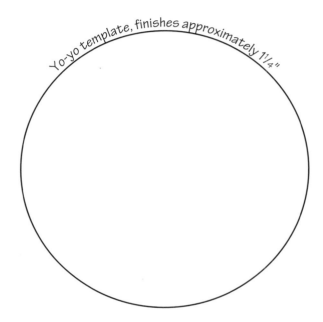

Yo-yo template, finishes approximately 1¼"

CERAMIC BUTTON SCOOP...

The charming ceramic buttons featured on this cardigan were designed by Debbie Mumm for Mill Hill. Look for these and many other delightful designs in your local quilt shop. If you are unable to find them, see page 40 for ordering information.

#43033	flying heart
#43065	tea cup
#43066	pincushion
#43067	fan
#43069	small heart

To protect ceramic buttons during laundering, cover buttons with Button Clams™. These button protectors are made from a soft, flexible plastic and are easy to use. See ordering information on page 40.

COLLECTOR BOXES

Whether you are a collector of boxes or use boxes
to store your collectibles, you will find these
decorative boxes fun and easy
to make. Embellish them
with yo-yos, doilies,
and buttons to add
a timeless hint of
romance. Make some
for yourself and
several to give away.

MATERIALS NEEDED

Round paper maché box with lid
Fabric
    8" or 10" box - ¼ yard (box)
      ⅓ yard (lid)
    6" box - ⅙ yard (box)
      ¼ yard (lid)
Heavyweight fusible web
    10" box - 1¼ yard
    8" box - 1 yard
    6" box - ⅞ yard
Yo-yos - Coordinated fabric scraps
Batting
Hot glue gun and glue sticks
Notions - Charms, doilies, decorative cording,
    ceramic and other assorted buttons

ASSEMBLY

1. Measure circumference and height of box.
   Draw rectangle on paper side of fusible web
   that is 1" larger than circumference by 2" larger
   than height. Cut out rectangle, approximately
   ¼" outside drawn line.

2. Refer to step 2 of Quick-Fuse Appliqué
   directions on page 40. Fuse to wrong side of
   fabric. Cut out rectangle on drawn line. Remove
   paper backing. Fuse fabric around box, leaving
   1" of fabric extending beyond both top and
   bottom.

3. Fold fabric to inside of box, fusing in place as
   you go. Cut slits, ½" apart, in fabric that
   extends beyond bottom
   of box. Fuse fabric
   to bottom.

4. To cover lid, trace
   around lid on paper
   side of fusible web.
   Draw second circle 1"
   outside first circle to
   make a ring.

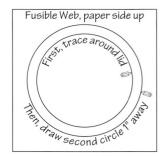

Fusible Web, paper side up

First, trace around lid

Then, draw second circle 1" away

5. Cut away fusible
   web on inside
   circle. Fuse to
   wrong side of lid
   fabric.

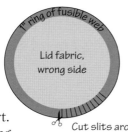

Lid fabric, wrong side

6. Cut out circle on
   outer line. Remove
   paper backing. There
   will now be a 1" ring
   of fusible web on
   wrong side of lid
   fabric. Cut 1" slits
   around edge of circle,
   approximately ½" apart.

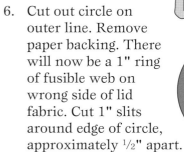

1" ring of fusible web

Lid fabric, wrong side

Cut slits around edge,
approximately ½" apart

7. Cut two pieces of batting
   the size of box lid. Place
   on top of lid. Center fabric
   circle, right side up, over lid and batting. Fuse to
   rim. Think of the lid as a clock and begin by
   fusing at the twelve o'clock position. Gently
   stretch and fuse at the six o'clock position.
   Continue to stretch and fuse at three o'clock,
   nine o'clock, and so on, until entire circle is
   fused to rim.

8. Measure circumference of lid. Draw rectangle
   on paper side of fusible web that is 1" larger
   than lid circumference by rim depth. Cut out
   rectangle, approximately ¼" outside drawn
   line, and fuse to wrong side of lid fabric. Cut
   out rectangle. Remove paper backing and fuse
   strip around rim.

9. Refer to Making Yo-yos on page 39. Make six
   to eight yo-yos using templates on page 7.
   Embellish lid with a cluster of assorted doilies,
   yo-yos, buttons, decorative cording, and charms.
   Glue in place. If desired, glue decorative cording
   around edge of lid.

CERAMIC BUTTON SCOOP...

The charming ceramic buttons featured on
these boxes were designed by Debbie Mumm
for Mill Hill. Look for these and many other
delightful designs in your local quilt shop.
If you are unable to find them, see page 40
for ordering information.

#43003	yellow cat
#43040	bee skep
#43066	pincushion
#43067	fan

SEWING IS MY CUP OF TEA

Has your favorite tea cup outlived its usefulness yet you still can't part with it? Enjoy its beauty once more by transforming it into an elegant, yet useful, pincushion.

MATERIALS NEEDED

Tea cup
4" Styrofoam ball
Fabric - ¼ yard
Yo-yos - Coordinated fabric scraps
Batting
Hot glue gun and glue sticks
Notions - Doily, ceramic button, decorative cording

ASSEMBLY

1. Measure diameter of tea cup. Cut fabric circle that is twice as big as tea cup diameter. Cut two batting circles the same size as tea cup diameter.

2. Place styrofoam ball in tea cup. Mark line around ball at rim of cup. Remove ball and cut one side off on drawn line to fit in tea cup.

3. Run a gathering stitch around edge of fabric circle. Place two batting circles on flat surface of styrofoam. Center fabric circle, right side up, over styrofoam and batting. Pull thread to gather fabric over styrofoam and batting. Knot thread.

4. Position and glue pincushion, flat side up, in cup.

5. Measure circumference of tea cup rim. Cut decorative cording 1" longer than measurement. Beginning and ending at tea cup handle, glue cording around rim, tucking ends down into cup.

6. Refer to Making Yo-yos on page 39. Make four yo-yos using large yo-yo template on page 7. Cluster doily, yo-yos, and ceramic button on top of pincushion. Glue in place.

BUTTON JAR LAMP

Create a charming button jar lamp with the warm glow of country. It's quick, it's easy, and oh, so fun to make.

MATERIALS NEEDED

Lamp shade
Appliqué pieces - Coordinated fabric scraps
Double sided adhesive
    We used PeelnStick™ by Therm O Web
Assorted buttons
Permanent, fine-point felt pen
Hot glue gun and glue sticks
Quart jar
Electric lamp adapter for quart jar
    See ordering information on page 40.

ASSEMBLY

1. Select design to adhere to lamp shade and make templates. We used 2" squares and the heart on page 7.

2. Trace around templates on plain side of PeelnStick™. Cut out designs, approximately ¼" outside drawn line. Peel away printed paper backing.

3. Apply sticky side of PeelnStick™ to wrong side of fabric. Cut out design and peel away remaining paper backing.

4. Position and stick design to lampshade. Use permanent felt pen to draw quilting stitches around designs. Position and glue buttons to lamp shade.

5. Fill quart jar with buttons and assemble lamp.

PILLOWS AT HEART

Finished Size: Approximately 8" x 10"

Share cherished buttons and bits of lace by making romantic country pillows for those you love. Embellish with stitching and stuff with care to create treasured heirlooms for generations to come.

MATERIALS NEEDED

(to make one pillow)

Fabric - Two 13" squares
Polyester fiberfill stuffing
Notions - Embroidery floss, ceramic and other assorted buttons, doilies, lace, decorative cording

ASSEMBLY

1. Trace Pillows At Heart pattern from page 38. Fold each fabric square in half with right sides together, pin pattern along folded edge, and cut out heart.
2. Stitch a saying such as "Bless your heart" on pillow front. Use three strands of embroidery floss and a back stitch, referring to Embroidery Stitch Guide on page 40.
3. Sew lace or doily to pillow front. If desired, weave decorative cording through holes of lace.
4. Pin pillow front to back with right sides together. Using ¼" seam, sew around edge, leaving an opening on one side for turning. Clip curves and inside point. Turn pillow right side out and press.
5. Sew assorted buttons to pillow front.
6. Stuff pillow and sew opening closed. Sew decorative cording around edge of pillow.

SMALL STUFFED HEARTS

Finished Size: Approximately 6" x 6"

Combine a touch of romance with a bit of country charm to create these quick and easy stuffed hearts. Hang them from a door knob, tuck them in a basket, or fill them with potpourri.

MATERIALS NEEDED

(to make one stuffed heart)

Fabric - Two 8½" squares
Polyester fiberfill stuffing
Yo-yos - Coordinated fabric scraps
Notions - Embroidery floss, ceramic and other assorted buttons, charms, doilies, decorative cording

ASSEMBLY

1. Trace Small Stuffed Heart pattern from page 38. Fold each fabric square in half with right sides together, pin pattern along folded edge, and cut out heart.
2. Stitch a saying such as "Bless your heart" on one heart. Use three strands of embroidery floss and a back stitch, referring to Embroidery Stitch Guide on page 40. Sew doily to heart.
3. Pin front to back with right sides together. Using ¼" seam, sew around edge, leaving an opening on one side for turning. Clip curves and inside point. Turn right side out and press.
4. Refer to Making Yo-yos on page 39. Make yo-yos using templates on pages 7 and 13. Sew assorted buttons and yo-yos to heart.
5. Stuff heart and sew opening closed. Sew decorative cording around edge of heart. If desired, make a hanger with decorative cording and sew to heart.

CERAMIC BUTTON SCOOP...

The charming ceramic buttons featured on the stuffed hearts were designed by Debbie Mumm for Mill Hill. Look for these and many other delightful designs in your local quilt shop. If you are unable to find them, see page 40 for ordering information.

#43024	button heart
#43065	tea cup
#43066	pincushion
#43067	fan
#43072	star garden angel

PILLOWS AT HEART
Cut two on fold

SMALL STUFFED HEART
Cut two on fold

Place on fold

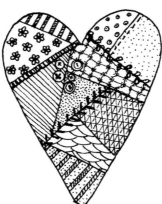

CRAZY-PIECED PILLOW
It is quick and easy to make an updated crazy quilt pillow. Refer to directions for Crazy-pieced Border on page 6 to make a 13" crazy-pieced square. Cut out heart. Add decorative stitching and buttons before sewing and stuffing pillow.

GENERAL DIRECTIONS

QUICK CORNER TRIANGLES

Quick corner triangles are formed by simply sewing fabric squares to other squares and rectangles. The directions and diagrams with each project show you what size pieces to use and where to place square on corresponding piece. See fabric key with each project for fabric identification. Follow steps 1–3 below to make corner triangle units.

1. With a pencil, draw diagonal line from corner to corner on wrong side of fabric square that will form the triangle. See Diagram A. This will be your sewing line.

2. With right sides together, place square on corresponding piece. Matching raw edges, pin in place and sew ON drawn diagonal line.

3. Press seam in direction of arrow as shown in step-by-step project diagram. Trim off excess fabric leaving ¹/₄" seam allowance as shown in Diagram B. Measure completed corner triangle unit to ensure greatest accuracy.

A.

Sewing line

B.

Trim ¹/₄" away from sewing line

C.

Finished corner triangle unit

MAKING YO-YOS

1. Make template of desired size yo-yo. Trace around template on wrong side of fabric and cut out on drawn line.

2. Thread needle and make a double knot at one end. Turning in a ¹/₈"–¹/₄" seam allowance as you go, sew running stitches close to folded edge. Stitches should be ¹/₈"– ³/₁₆" long.

3. When you reach your beginning point, gather stitches tightly to close circle. Smooth and flatten yo-yo so the hole is in the center. Knot and cut off excess gathering thread.

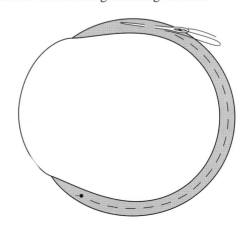

LAYERING THE QUILT

1. Cut backing and batting pieces 4"–6" larger than quilt top.

2. Lay pressed backing on bottom (right side down), batting in the middle, and pressed quilt top on top. Make sure everything is centered and that backing and batting are flat. Backing and batting should extend 2"–3" beyond quilt top.

3. Begin basting in center and work toward outer edges. Baste vertically and horizontally, forming a 3"– 4" grid. Baste or pin completely around edge of quilt top. Trim batting and backing to ¹/₄" from raw edge of quilt top.

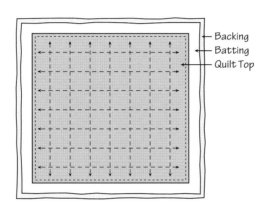

BINDING THE QUILT

1. Fold and press binding strips in half lengthwise with wrong sides together.

2. With raw edges even, lay binding strips on top and bottom edges of quilt top. Sew through all layers, ¹/₄" from quilt edge. Press binding away from the quilt top. Trim excess length of binding.

3. Sew remaining two binding strips to quilt sides. Press and trim excess length.

4. Folding top and bottom first, fold binding around to back. Press and pin in position. Hand stitch binding in place.

← Fold top & bottom binding in first

QUICK-FUSE APPLIQUÉ

Quick-fuse appliqué is a method of adhering appliqué pieces to a background with fusible web. For quick and easy results, simply quick-fuse appliqué pieces in place. Use a non-sewable, heavyweight fusible web such as *HeatnBond Ultrahold*. For some projects, finishing edges of appliqué pieces with a hand or machine stitch may be desired. Use a sewable, lightweight fusible web, such as *HeatnBond Lite*, for these projects. Laundering is not recommended unless edges are finished.

1. With paper side up, lay fusible web over appliqué design. Leaving ¹⁄₂" space between pieces, trace all elements of design. Trace design details, such as eyes, mouths, and lettering, with the appropriate piece. Cut around traced pieces, approximately ¹⁄₄" outside the tracing line. See Diagram A.

    Fusible Web

2. With paper side up, position and iron fusible web to wrong side of selected fabrics. Follow manufacturer's directions for iron temperature and fusing time. Cut out each piece on traced line. See Diagram B.

    Fabric - wrong side

3. Transfer traced design details to fabric side of pieces with a permanent, fine-point felt pen such as a *Pigma Micron* pen by Sakura. If you are uncomfortable using a permanent felt pen, trace lightly with a pencil first. It may be helpful to use a light table for this step.

4. Remove paper backing from pieces. A thin film will remain on the wrong side. Position and fuse all pieces of one appliqué design at a time onto background, referring to color photo for placement. We found it helpful to use The Appliqué Pressing Sheet™ by Bear Thread Designs to easily position the Dresden Plate. See ordering information at right.

Note: Every attempt has been made to provide clear, concise, and accurate instructions. We used the quick cutting and sewing methods most appropriate for you to successfully complete these projects. Other techniques may also achieve the same results.

EMBROIDERY STITCH GUIDE

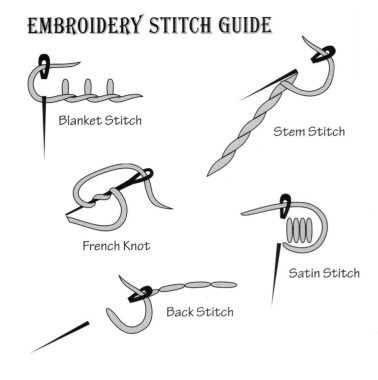

Blanket Stitch

Stem Stitch

French Knot

Satin Stitch

Back Stitch

MAIL ORDER SOURCES

Ceramic Buttons
Mill Hill, a division of
Gay Bowles Sales, Inc.
PO Box 1060
Janesville, WI 53547
(800)356-9438

The Appliqué Pressing Sheet™
Product #206
Bear Thread Designs
Route 1, Box 1640
Belgrade, MO 63622
(573)766-5695

The Button Clam™
1¹⁄₂" Button Clam–#BIT-015/B4
2" Button Clam–#BIT-020/B4
A Little Bit of This & That, Inc.
Route 1, Box 524 AB
Bonners Ferry, ID 83805
(208)267-2801

Electric Lamp Adapter for Quart Jar
Item #720–zinc lid
Item #441–wood lid
Mathews Wire
654 W. Morrison
Frankfort, IN 46041
(800)826-9650